This Book Belongs To:

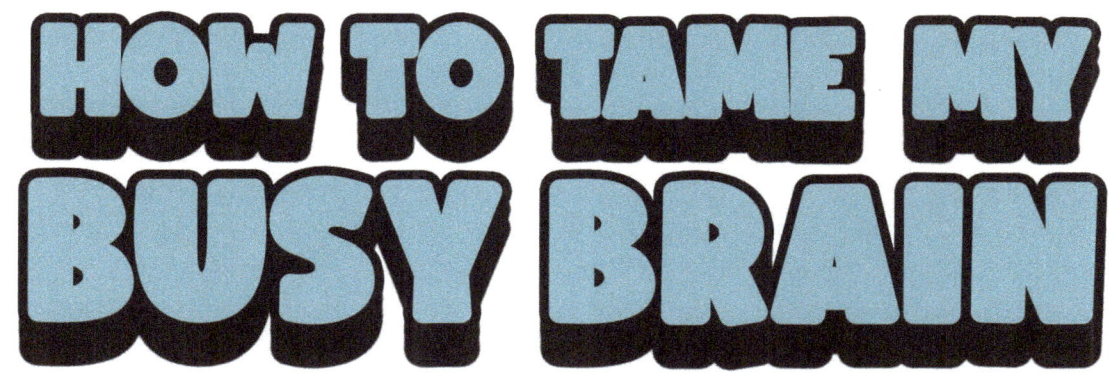

HOW TO TAME MY BUSY BRAIN

WRITTEN BY KRISTY HIGH

ILLUSTRATION BY ZURI BOOK PROS

Copyright © 2021 by Kristy High.

All rights reserved. This book or any portion thereof may not be reproduced or used in any manner whatsoever without the express written permission of the publisher except for the use of brief quotations in a book review.

Printed in the United States of America.
First printing, 2021.
ISBN (Paperback) 978-0-578-91514-2

Dedication

This book is dedicated to kids everywhere that suffer from fear, worry and anxiety.
There is nothing wrong with you. Be brave, speak up and tell others how you feel.

Hi, my name is Sam. There are a lot of things I like doing. I like riding my bike with my friends, helping my dad in the kitchen, and going to the park. One thing I don't like is worrying. Sometimes I worry that I'll get left behind at the park. Sometimes I worry that when my dog runs off he won't come back. Sometimes I worry that I'll get a bad grade on a test. When I get worried I feel sad, and mad, and sick all at once.

The first time that this happened to me I was playing at my friend Nick's house. Nick's dad made lemonade for everyone, and when he handed me my glass it slipped out of my hand. The glass broke and there was lemonade everywhere! I said that I was "sorry", and offered to help clean it up.

Nick's dad said that it was okay as he picked up the broken glass and mopped up the lemonade. He said that everyone makes mistakes sometimes. Even though he said that, I felt very bad. I didn't feel like playing anymore. I felt like Nick's parents would never let me come over again.

I worried that Nick would tell everyone at school what had happened and they would make fun of me. I still felt bad that night when I went home for dinner. I didn't even want to eat my pizza, and pizza is my favorite!

The last time this happened was after soccer practice last week. My mom was thirty minutes late picking me up. She called my coach, and he stayed behind to sit with me, but I still felt worried. My mom is never late to get me after soccer practice. In fact, most of the time she's early and she sits and waits until practice is over.

When my mom did arrive she was in a bad mood, she said there had been a lot of traffic on the way. I tried to be quiet but my mom could tell something was wrong, and when we got home she asked me about it.

"Was everything okay at practice?" She asked.
Everything had been fine at practice, I even scored two goals but I wasn't sure if it was okay to be happy about that.
"It was fine mom," I said.
She told me that I didn't look like everything was fine and asked me if I was feeling well.

I told her that my stomach hurt, and my head hurt, and my palms were feeling sweaty. She asked me how long I had been feeling that way. I told her that it had started when I found out she was going to be late to pick me up after practice.
"Have you ever felt this way before," she asked.
"Sometimes," I told her, "But it always goes away."

It was then that she told me she was going to call Dr. Barnes and make an appointment. That made me worry too, but then mom hugged me and told me it was going to be okay.

A few days later we went to see Dr. Barnes. He took my temperature, weighed me, listened to my heart and asked me to tell him how I was feeling. I told him that I was feeling fine, but then my mom told him about the day after soccer practice. He asked me if I had ever felt that way before and I told him the same thing I told my mom. It was then that he suggested to my mom that we go see his friend Dr. Hernandez.

Dr. Hernandez had a different kind of office than Dr. Barnes. She didn't take my temperature or weigh me, or listen to my heart. Instead she talked to me. She asked me to tell her about how I felt when I was worried, and then she asked me to tell her when I felt that way. According to Dr. Hernandez what I feel is called anxiety.

"Is something wrong with me?" I asked her, my stomach was starting to hurt.
"Not at all, a lot of people, even grownups, get anxious sometimes," she told me.
"Is there any way to make it go away?" I asked.
Dr. Hernandez told me that she could teach me and my parents some ways to help me handle being anxious.

"Will these things stop me from worrying," I asked.
"They will not stop you from worrying," she said, "but they should help you to feel less worried."
I wanted to feel less worried.

One of the activities Dr. Hernandez suggested was looking at a situation in a different way. One situation I told her I was worried about was giving the wrong answer in class. She said that when that happens that I should remember that everyone makes mistakes sometimes, and that making a mistake and being corrected is another way to learn.

Another activity she suggested was to write down what I'm feeling or to draw a picture about it. She said this can help me to get out what I'm feeling, and that I may want to keep a journal or a sketch book.

Dr. Hernandez also told my parents to make sure that I was getting enough sleep, and enough time to play. She said that regular things like these along with making sure I drank water and had time to relax are good ways to make sure that my feeling anxious isn't taking over.

I still feel anxious and I still don't like it. I still feel sad, mad, and sick all at once, but with the tips Dr. Hernandez gave me and my parents I'm able to feel this way less. I'm so glad I told my mom what I was feeling.

Activity for Kids

Everyone worries and gets anxious. What are you worried about today? Parents have your child list their worries on a piece of paper. Get an empty shoe box that will be used as the "**worry**" box. Talk with them about why they are feeling this way. After the discussion, put the paper in the box and close it. Let your child know that they are leaving the worries inside! Do this as often as needed adding the worries to the box each time.

About The Author

Kristy High, M.Ed. is an award-winning author and in-demand publicist, author coach and health educator. She is the 3x co-author of the acclaimed children's books, *Peter's Perfect Pipes, I'm No Different Than You* and *I am Powerful, I am Amazing, I am a King*. Kristy is passionate about education, reading and literacy and encourages children to be the best version of themselves. As someone who has suffered with worry and anxiety since childhood, Kristy wanted to write a book that brings awareness to childhood anxiety and takes away the stigma of discussing mental health issues.

www.ingramcontent.com/pod-product-compliance
Lightning Source LLC
Chambersburg PA
CBHW061801290426
44109CB00030B/2917